Formatting

Easy Excel Essentials
Volume 5

M.L. HUMPHREY

Copyright © 2017-2018 M.L. Humphrey

All rights reserved.

ISBN: 978-1-950902-34-7

Also published under ISBN 978-1720564157

TITLES BY M.L. HUMPHREY

EASY EXCEL ESSENTIALS
Pivot Tables
Conditional Formatting
Charts
The IF Functions
Formatting
Printing

EXCEL ESSENTIALS
Excel for Beginners
Intermediate Excel
50 Useful Excel Functions
50 More Excel Functions

EXCEL ESSENTIALS QUIZ BOOKS
The Excel for Beginners Quiz Book
The Intermediate Excel Quiz Book
The 50 Useful Excel Functions Quiz Book
The 50 More Excel Functions Quiz Book

DATA PRINCIPLES
Data Principles for Beginners

BUDGETING FOR BEGINNERS
Budgeting for Beginners
Excel for Budgeting

WORD ESSENTIALS
Word for Beginners
Intermediate Word

MAIL MERGE
Mail Merge for Beginners

POWERPOINT ESSENTIALS
PowerPoint for Beginners

.

CONTENTS

INTRODUCTION

In *Excel for Beginners* I covered the basics of working in Excel, including how to format in Excel and how to print. In *Intermediate Excel* I covered a number of intermediate-level topics such as pivot tables, charts, and conditional formatting. And in *50 Useful Excel Functions* I covered fifty of the most useful functions you can use in Excel.

But I realize that some users will just want to know about a specific topic and not buy a guide that covers a variety of other topics that aren't of interest to them.

So this series of guides is meant to address that need. Each guide in the series covers one specific topic such as pivot tables, conditional formatting, or charts.

I'm going to assume in these guides that you have a basic understanding of how to navigate Excel, although each guide does include an Appendix with a brief discussion of basic terminology to make sure that we're on the same page.

The guides are written using Excel 2013, which should be similar enough for most users of Excel to follow, but anyone using a version of Excel prior to Excel 2007 probably won't be able to use them effectively.

Also, keep in mind that the content in these guides is drawn from *Excel for Beginners, Intermediate Excel,* and/or *50 Useful Excel Functions,* so if you think you'll end up buying more than one or two of these guides you're probably better off just buying *Excel for Beginners, Intermediate Excel,* and/or *50 Useful Excel Functions.*

With that said, let's talk Formatting.

FORMATTING

Below is an alphabetical listing of the various formatting options available for cells within Excel. You can either format one cell at a time by highlighting that specific cell and then choosing your formatting option or you can format multiple cells at once by highlighting all of them and then choosing the formatting option.

What you'll see below is that there are basically two main ways to format cells in current versions of Excel. You can either use the Home tab and click on the option you want from there or you can right-click and select the Format Cells option from the dropdown menu. (You can also use Ctrl + 1 to access the Format Cells dialogue box.)

There are also shortcut keys available for things like bolding (Ctrl + B), italicizing (Ctrl + I), and underlining (Ctrl +U) text that give you a third option. These are my preferred choice and at least those three are worth memorizing.

For those of you using older versions of Excel (pre-2007) you'll need to use the Ctrl shortcuts and/or the Format Cells dialogue box options since the Home tab options didn't exist in older versions of Excel.

Aligning Your Text Within a Cell

By default, text within a cell is left-aligned and bottom-aligned. But at times you may want to adjust this. I often will center text or top-align my entries because they look better to me that way.

To change a cell's alignment, highlight the cell(s) you want to change and go to the Alignment section on the Home tab.

You'll see on the left-hand side of that section six different images with lines in them. These are visual representations of your possible choices.

The first row has the top aligned, middle aligned, and bottom aligned options. You can choose one of these three options for your cell.

The second row has the left-aligned, centered, and right-aligned options. You can also choose one of these three options for your cell.

So you can have a cell with top-aligned and centered text or top-aligned and right-aligned, etc.

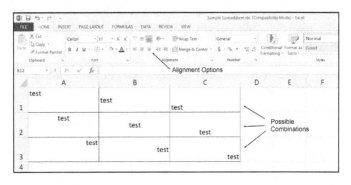

The angled "ab" with an arrow under it in the top row of the Alignment section also has a handful of pre-defined options for changing the direction of text within a cell.

You can choose to Angle Counterclockwise, Angle Clockwise, Vertical Text, Rotate Text Up, and Rotate Text Down.

(It also offers another way to access the Alignment tab of the Format Cells dialogue box which we'll talk about next. Just click on Format Cell Alignment at the bottom of the dropdown menu.)

* * *

Another way to change the text alignment within a cell(s) is to highlight your cell(s) and then right-click and choose Format Cells from the dropdown menu.

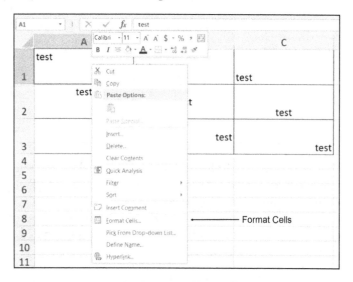

When the Format Cells dialogue box opens, go to the Alignment tab, which is the second option.

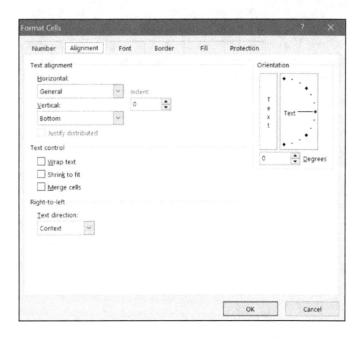

Choose from the Horizontal and Vertical dropdown menus to change the position of text within a cell (Top, Center, Bottom, Left, Right, etc.).

The Horizontal and Vertical dropdown menus also have a few additional choices (like Justify and Distributed), but you generally shouldn't need them.

(And be wary of Fill which it seems will repeat whatever you have in that cell over and over again until it fills the cell. Remember, if you do something you don't like, Ctrl + Z.)

You can also change the orientation of your text so that it's vertical or angled by entering the number of degrees (90 to make it vertical) or by clicking to move the line within the Orientation box on the right-hand side to where you want it.

Bolding Text

You can bold text in a number of ways.

First, you can highlight the cell(s) you want bolded and click on the large capital B in the Font section of the Home tab.

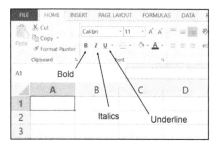

Second, you can highlight the cell(s) you want bolded and then type Ctrl and B at the same time. (Ctrl + B)

Or, third, you can highlight the cell(s) you want to bold and then right-click and choose Format Cells from the dropdown menu. Once you're in the Format Cells dialogue box, go to the Font tab and choose Bold from the Font Style options. If you want text that is both bolded and italicized, choose Bold Italic.

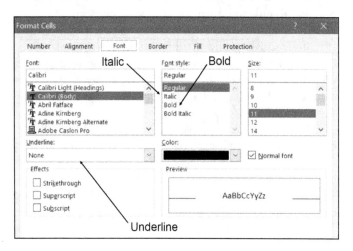

You can also bold just part of the text in a cell by clicking into the cell, highlighting the portion of the text that you want to bold, and then using any of the above methods.

To remove bolding from text or cells that already have it, highlight the bolded portion and then type Ctrl + B, or click on the large capital B in the Font section of the Home tab, or go back to the Format Cells dialogue box and change your selection to Regular.

(If you happen to highlight text that is only partially bolded you will have to use Ctrl + B or click on the large capital B twice to remove the bold formatting because the first time will apply the formatting to the entire selection.)

Borders Around Cells

It's nice to have borders around your data to keep the information in each cell distinct, especially if you're going to print your document.

There are two main ways to add borders around a cell or set of cells.

First, you can highlight the cells you want to place a border around and then go to the Font section on the Home tab and choose from the Borders dropdown option. It's a four-square grid with an arrow next to it that's located between the U used for underlining and the color bucket used for filling a cell with color. Click on the arrow to see your available options, and then choose the type of border you want.

(If you just want a simple border all around the cells and between multiple cells click on the All Borders option.)

With this option, to adjust the line thickness or line colors, see the options in the Draw Borders section, but be sure to choose your colors and line style before you choose your border type because the color and line type you choose will only apply to borders you draw after you choose them.

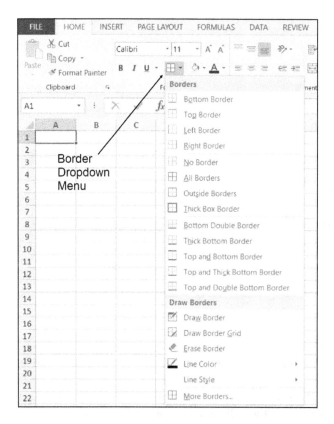

You can combine border types to get the appearance you want. For example, you could choose All Borders for the entire set of cells and then Thick Box Border to put a darker outline around the perimeter, something I do often.

Your second choice is to highlight the cells where you want to place a border and then right-click and select Format Cells from the dropdown menu. Next, go to the Border tab, the fourth tab in the dialogue box, and choose your border style, type, and color from there.

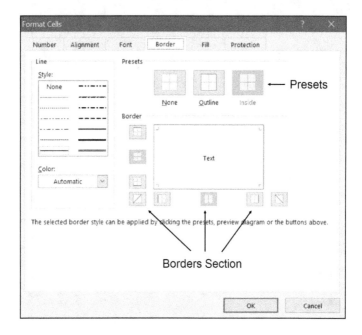

If you want one of the Preset options (outline or inside lines), just click on it. To clear what you've done and start over you can select None from the Presets section.

If you want only a subset of lines (for example, only the bottom of the cell to have a line), click on the choice you want from the Border section around the Text box. You can click on more than one of the lines in this section. So you could have, for example, a top and bottom border, but nothing else.

And, if you want to change the style of a line or its color from the default, you should do so in the Line section on the left-hand side before you select where you want your lines to appear. The format you choose will only apply to lines you insert after you make that choice.

This is also the only place where you can insert a diagonal line into a cell.

You can see what you've chosen and what it will look like in the sample box in the center of the screen.

Coloring a Cell (Fill Color)

You can color (or fill) an entire cell with almost any color you want. To do this, highlight the cell(s) you want to color, go to the Font section of the Home tab, and click on the arrow to the right of the paint bucket that has a yellow line under it. This should bring up a colors menu with 70 different colors to choose from, including many that are arranged as complementary themes. If you want one of those colors, just click on it.

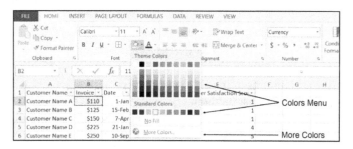

If none of those colors work for you, or you need to use a specific corporate color, click on More Colors at the bottom. This will bring up the Colors dialogue box.

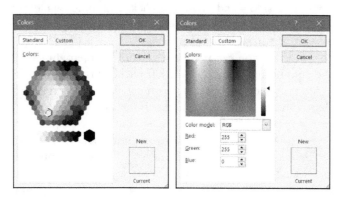

The first tab of the Colors dialogue box looks like a honeycomb and has a number of colors you can choose from by clicking into the honeycomb. The second tab is the Custom tab. It has a rainbow of colors that you can click on and also allows you to enter specific red, green, and blue values to get the exact color you need. (If you have a corporate color palette, they should give you the RGB values for each of the colors. At least my last employer did.)

On the Custom tab, you can also use the arrow on the right-hand side to darken or lighten your color.

With both tabs, you can see the color you've chosen in the bottom right corner. If you like your choice, click on OK. If you don't want to add color to a cell after all, choose Cancel.

Column Width (Adjusting)

If your columns aren't the width you want, you have three options for adjusting them.

First, you can right-click on the column and choose Column Width from the dropdown menu. When the box showing you the current column width appears, enter a new column width.

Second, you can place your cursor to the right side of the column name—it should look like a line with arrows on either side—and then left-click and hold while you move the cursor to the right or the left until the column is as wide as you want it to be.

Or, third, you can place your cursor on the right side of the column name and double left-click. This will make the column as wide or as narrow as the widest text currently in that column. (Usually. Sometimes this one has a mind of its own.)

To adjust all column widths in your document at once to the width of the text within each of your columns, you can highlight the entire worksheet and then double-left click on any column border and it will adjust each column to the contents in that column.

(Usually. See comment above.)

To have uniform column widths throughout your worksheet, highlight the whole worksheet, right-click on a column, choose Column Width, and set your column width.

Highlighting the whole worksheet and then left-clicking and dragging one column to the desired width will also work.

Currency Formatting

If you type a number into a cell in Excel, it'll just show that number. So, 25 is 25. $25 is $25. But sometimes you want those numbers to display as currency with the dollar sign and cents showing, too. Or you've already copied in unformatted numbers and now want them to have the same currency format.

To do this, highlight the cell(s) you want formatted this way, and then go to the Number section of the Home tab, and click on the $ sign.

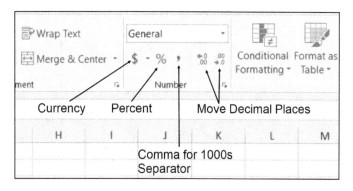

Another option is to highlight the cells you want formatted that way, go to the Number section of the Home tab, and use the dropdown to choose either Currency or Accounting. (The $ symbol applies Accounting formatting, but I often prefer Currency formatting.)

You can also highlight the cell(s), right-click, choose the Format Cells option, go to the Number tab, and choose either Currency or Accounting from there.

Date Formatting

Sometimes Excel has a mind of its own about how to format dates. For example, if I type in 1/1 for January 1st, Excel will show it as 1-Jan. It means the same thing, but if I would rather it display as 1/1/2017, I need to change the formatting.

To do this, click on the cell with your date in it, go to the Number section on the Home tab, click on the dropdown menu, and choose Short Date. (You can also choose Long Date if you prefer that format.)

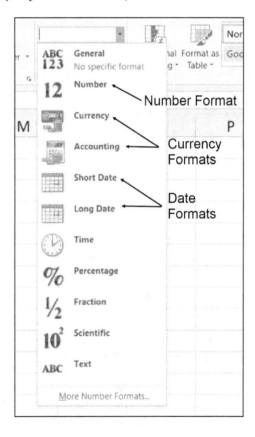

Another option is to highlight your cell(s), right click, choose Format Cells from the dropdown menu, go to the Number tab of the Format Cells dialogue box, and choose your date format from there by clicking on Date and then selecting one of the numerous choices it provides.

Note that if you just enter a month and day of the month like I did above, Excel will default to assuming that you meant the date to be for the current year and will store your date as MM-DD-YYYY even if you weren't trying to specify a year.

Excel always assigns a year to dates, so be sure that you put the correct year when you enter your data.

Font Choice and Size

In my version of Excel the default font choice is Calibri and the default font size is 11 point. You may have strong preferences about what font you use or work for a company that uses specific fonts for its brand or just want some variety in terms of font size or type within a specific document. In that case, you will need to change your font and/or your font size.

There are two ways to do this.

First, you can highlight the cells you want to change or the specific text you want to change, and go to the Font section on the Home tab. Select a different font or font size from the dropdown menus there.

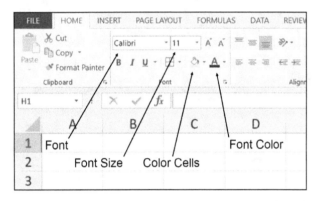

You also have the option to increase or decrease the font one size at a time by clicking on the A's with little arrows that are to the right of the font size dropdown box.

You can also just click into the font or font size boxes and type in what you want. For font, as soon as you start typing it will take you to that portion of the listed fonts. (So T takes me to Tahoma.) For font size, just type in the exact font size you want. You can use sizes that are not listed in the dropdown menu.

Your other option for changing font or font size is to highlight the cells or text you want to change, go to the Format Cells dialogue box (Ctrl + 1 or right-click and choose Format Cells), and then go to the Font tab and choose your Font and Size from the listed values.

You can choose a font size that isn't listed by clicking into the font size box and typing the value you want.

Font Color

The default color for all text in Excel is black, but you can change that if you want or need to. (For example, if you've colored a cell with a darker color you may want to consider changing the font color to white to make the text in that cell more visible.)

You have two options. First, you can highlight the cells or the specific text you want to change, go to the Font section on the Home tab, and click on the arrow next to the A with a red line under it (see image above). You can then choose from one of the 70 colors that are listed.

If those aren't enough of a choice you can click on More Colors and select your color from the Colors dialogue box. (See Coloring a Cell for more detail about that option.)

Second, you can highlight the cell or text, go to the Format Cells dialogue box (Ctrl + 1), go to the Font tab, and then click on the dropdown menu under Color which will bring up the same seventy color options as well as the ability to choose More Colors and add a custom color.

Italicizing Text

You do this by highlighting the cell(s) you want italicized and clicking on the slanted I in the Font section on the Home tab (see image under the Bolding description), or by highlighting the cell(s) and holding down the Ctrl key and the I key at the same time (Ctrl + I).

Or, you can highlight the cell(s), go to Font tab of the Format Cells dialogue box (Ctrl + 1), and choose Italic from the Font Style options. (See image under the Bolding description.)

You can also italicize just part of the text in a cell by only selecting that portion and then using one of the methods above.

To remove italics from text or cells that already have it, you follow the exact same steps. (Highlight your selection and then use Ctrl + I or click on the slanted I in the Font section on the Home tab. Or go back to the Format Cells dialogue box and change your selection to Regular from Italic.)

If you select text that was partially formatted with italics and partially not then you'll need to use Ctrl + I or click on the slanted I twice to remove the italics because the first time will apply italics to the entire selection.

Merge & Center

Merge and Center is a specialized command that can come in handy when you're working with a table where you want a header that spans multiple columns of data. (Don't use it if you plan to do a lot of data analysis with what you've input into the worksheet because it will mess with your ability to filter, sort, or use pivot tables. It's really for creating a finalized, pretty-looking report.)

If you're going to merge and center text, make sure that the text you want to keep is in the top-most and left-most of the cells you plan to merge and center. Data in the other cells that are being merged will be deleted. (You'll get a warning message to this effect if you have values in any of the other cells.)

You can merge cells across columns and down rows. So you could, for example, merge four cells that span two columns and two rows into one big cell while keeping all of the other cells in those columns and rows separate.

To Merge & Center, highlight all of the cells you want to merge, go to the Alignment section of the Home tab, and choose Merge & Center. This will combine your selected cells into one cell and center the contents from the topmost, left-most cell that was merged across the newly created merged cell.

You'll see on that dropdown that you can also choose to just Merge Across (which will just merge the cells in the first row) or to Merge Cells (which will merge the cells but won't center the text).

Also, if you ever need to unmerge those merged cells you can do so by selecting the Unmerge Cells option from that dropdown.

You can also Merge Cells by highlighting the cells, going to the Alignment tab of the Format Cells dialogue box (Ctrl + 1 or right-click and choose Format Cells), and then choosing to Merge Cells from there. If you use this option, you'll have to center the text separately.

Number Formatting

Sometimes when you copy data into Excel it doesn't format it the way you want. For example, I have a report I receive that includes ISBN numbers which are 10- or 13-digit numbers. When I copy those into Excel, it sometimes displays them in Scientific Number format (9.78E+12) as opposed to as a normal number, so I have to reformat those cells to display as numbers instead.

To change the formatting of your data to a number format, you have two options.

First, you can highlight the cell(s) and go to the Number section of the Home tab. From the drop-down menu choose Number. (Sometimes General will work as well.)

Excel will convert your entry to a number with two decimal places. So 100.00 instead of 100. You can then use the zeroes with arrows next to them that are below the drop-down box to adjust how many decimal places display. The one with the right-pointing arrow will reduce the number of decimal places. The one with the left-pointing arrow will increase them.

(See the Currency Formatting section for an image.)

Second, you can highlight the cell(s), right-click, go to the Number tab in the Format Cells dialogue box (Ctrl + 1 or right-click Format Cells), choose Number on the left-hand side, and then in the middle, choose your number of decimal places. There you can also choose whether to use a comma to separate out your thousands and millions and how to display negative numbers.

Percent Formatting

To format numbers as a percentage, highlight the cell(s), and click on the percent sign in the Number section of the Home tab.

You can also go to the Number tab in the Format Cells dialogue box and choose Percentage on the left-hand side. In the middle choose your number of decimal places.

Row Height (Adjusting)

If your rows aren't the correct height, you have three options for adjusting them.

First, you can right-click on the row you want to adjust, choose Row Height from the dropdown menu, and when the box showing you the current row height appears, enter a new row height.

Second, you can place your cursor along the lower border of the row number until it looks like a line with arrows above and below. Left-click and hold while you move the cursor up or down until the row is as tall as you want it to be.

Third, you can place your cursor along the lower border of the row, and double left-click. This will fit the row height to the text in the cell. (Usually.)

To adjust all row heights in your document at once to the height of the contents in each cell, you can highlight the entire worksheet and then double-left click on any row border and it will adjust each row to the contents in each individual row. (Usually. It doesn't always work when cells have lots of text in them.)

To have uniform row heights throughout your worksheet, you can highlight the whole sheet, right-click on a row, choose Row Height and set your row height that way.

Or you can select the entire worksheet, right-click on the border below a row, and adjust that row to the height you want for all rows.

Underlining Text

You have three options for underlining text.

First, you can highlight the cell(s) you want underlined and click on the underlined U in the Font section on the Home tab.

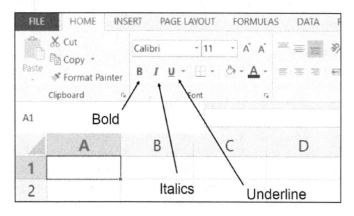

Second, you can highlight the cell(s) and type Ctrl and U at the same time. (Ctrl + U)

Third, you can highlight the cell(s), go to the Font tab in the Format Cells dialogue box (Ctrl + 1 or right-click Format Cells), and choose the type of underlining you want.

With the Format Cells dialogue box you have the options to choose single, double, single accounting, or double accounting as your type of underline. With Ctrl + U you just get a single underline. With the U in the Home tab you can use the dropdown arrow to get a double underline in addition to the single underline you get when you click on the U.

You can apply underlining to just part of the text in a cell by clicking into the cell, highlighting the portion of the text that you want to underline, and then using any of the above methods.

To remove underlining from text or cells that already have it, highlight the text and then use one of the above options. If you use the Format Cells dialogue box, change the selection to None.

If you use Ctrl + U or the U in the Home tab you may have to use them multiple times to remove all of the formatting. A double underline will convert to a single underline first. And, as with italics and bolding, if text was partially formatted the first use will apply the formatting to the whole selection and the second use will remove the formatting from the whole selection.

Wrapping Text

Sometimes you want to read all of the text in a cell, but you don't want that column to be wide enough to display all of the text. This is where the Wrap Text option becomes useful, because it will keep your text within the width of the column and display it on multiple lines by "wrapping" the text.

(Excel does have a limit as to how many rows of text it will display in one cell, so if you have any cells with lots of text in them, check to make sure that the full contents of the cell are actually visible. You may have to manually adjust the row height to see all of the text. Double-clicking does not work when this happens, so you need to click and drag or use the right-click option to change your row height to show all of the text.)

To Wrap Text in a cell, select the cell(s), go to the Alignment section of the Home Tab, and click on the Wrap Text option in the Alignment section.

Or you can highlight the cell(s), go to the Alignment tab in the Format Cells dialogue box (Ctrl + 1), and choose Wrap Text under Text Control.

One final formatting trick to share with you that is incredibly handy. (Maybe more so in Word than in Excel, but I use it frequently in both.)

Copying Formatting From One Cell To Another

In addition to the specific formatting options discussed above, if you already have a cell formatted the way you want it, you can copy the formatting from that cell to other cells you want formatted the same way.

You do this by using the Format Painter in the Clipboard section of the Home tab.

To do so highlight the cell(s) that have the formatting you want to copy (if the formatting is identical, just highlight one cell), click on the Format Painter, and then click into the cell(s) you want to copy the formatting to.

The contents in the destination cell will remain the same, but the font, font color, font size, cell borders, italics, bolding, underlining, text alignment, and text orientation will all change to match that of the cell that you swept the formatting from. If you sweep an entire column or row's formatting, the column width or row height will also change to match your selection.

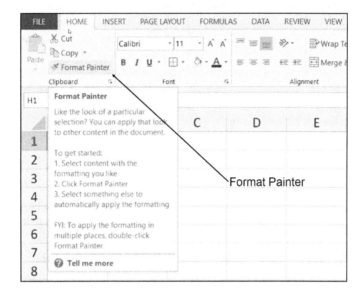

Format Painter

You need to be careful using the format sweeper because it will change *all* formatting in your destination cells. So, if the cell you're copying the formatting from is bolded and has red text, both of those attributes will copy over even if all you were trying to do was copy the bold formatting.

(This is more of a problem when using the tool in Word than in Excel, but it's still something to watch out for especially if you have borders around cells.)

Also, the tool copies formatting to whatever cell you select next, which can be a problem if the cell you're copying from isn't next to the one you're copying to. Do not use arrow keys to navigate between the cells. You need to immediately click into the cell you're transferring the formatting to after you click on the Format Painter.

(Remember, Ctrl + Z is your friend if you make a mistake.)

If you have more than one isolated cell that you need to apply formatting to, you can double-click the Format Painter and it will continue to copy the formatting of the original cell to every other cell you click on until you click on the Format Painter again or hit Esc to turn it off.

(You'll know the tool is still in operation because there will be a little broom next to your cursor.)

You can copy formatting from multiple cells to multiple cells, so say the formatting for an entire row to an entire other row, but be sure to double-check the results since this is much more likely to result in unintended formatting.

Also, you can copy formatting from one cell to multiple cells at a time by simply highlighting all of the cells you want to copy the formatting to at once.

If you format sweep and then undo, you'll see that the cell(s) you were trying to format from are surrounded by a dotted border as if you had copied the cells. Be sure to hit the Esc key before you continue.

CONCLUSION

So that was basic formatting. As you can see, in newer versions of Excel you have a lot of ways to do the same thing. That's because they kept the legacy approaches while adding in new ones.

I do think it's worth it to learn the Ctrl shortcuts for bolding, italics, and underlining. Also, I had never done so until recently but the Ctrl shortcut for accessing the Format Cells dialogue box (Ctrl + 1) is another handy one, although you may not use it often enough for it to be worthwhile, especially if you have a newer version of Excel where you can use the Home tab for most of your formatting needs.

Don't forget to put borders if you're going to print your worksheets. Those lines that you see on your screen don't show up when a document is printed, so that formatting option is incredibly valuable in my opinion.

And, as always, if you get stuck reach out and I'll try to help.

Good luck with it!

APPENDIX A: BASIC TERMINOLOGY

Column

Excel uses columns and rows to display information. Columns run across the top of the worksheet and, unless you've done something funky with your settings, are identified using letters of the alphabet.

Row

Rows run down the side of the worksheet and are numbered starting at 1 and up to a very high number.

Cell

A cell is a combination of a column and row that is identified by the letter of the column it's in and the number of the row it's in. For example, Cell A1 is the cell in the first column and first row of a worksheet.

Click

If I tell you to click on something, that means to use your mouse (or trackpad) to move the arrow on the screen over to a specific location and left-click or right-click on the option. (See the next definition for the difference between left-click and right-click).

If you left-click, this selects the item. If you right-click, this generally creates a dropdown list of options to choose from. If I don't tell you which to do, left- or right-click, then left-click.

Left-click/Right-click

If you look at your mouse or your trackpad, you generally have two flat buttons to press. One is on the left side, one is on the right. If I say left-click that means to press down on the button on the left. If I say right-click that means press down on the button on the right. (If you're used to using Word or Excel you may already do this without even thinking about it. So, if that's the case then think of left-click as what you usually use to select text and right-click as what you use to see a menu of choices.)

Spreadsheet

I'll try to avoid using this term, but if I do use it, I'll mean your entire Excel file. It's a little confusing because it can sometimes also be used to mean a specific worksheet, which is why I'll try to avoid it as much as possible.

Worksheet

This is the term I'll use as much as possible. A worksheet is a combination of rows and columns that you can enter data in. When you open an Excel file, it opens to worksheet one.

Formula Bar

This is the long white bar at the top of the screen with the $f\chi$ symbol next to it.

Tab

I refer to the menu choices at the top of the screen (File, Home, Insert, Page Layout, Formulas, Data, Review, and View) as tabs. Note how they look like folder tabs from an old-time filing system when selected? That's why.

Data

I use data and information interchangeably. Whatever information you put into a worksheet is your data.

Select

If I tell you to "select" cells, that means to highlight them.

Arrow

If I say that you can "arrow" to something that just means to use the arrow keys to navigate from one cell to another.

A1:A25

If I'm going to reference a range of cells, I'll use the shorthand notation that Excel uses in its formulas. So, for example, A1:A25 will mean Cells A1 through A25. If you ever don't understand exactly what I'm referring to, you can type it into a cell in Excel using the $=$ sign and see what cells Excel highlights. So, $=$A1:A25 should highlight cells A1 through A25 and $=$A1:B25 should highlight the cells in columns A and B and rows 1 through 25.

With Formulas Visible

Normally Excel doesn't show you the formula in a cell unless you click on that cell and then you only see the formula in the formula bar. But to help you see what I'm referring to, some of the screenshots in this guide will be provided with formulas visible. All this means is that I clicked on Show Formulas on the Formulas tab so that you could see what cells have formulas in them and what those formulas are.

Unless you do the same, your worksheet will not look like that. That's okay. Because you don't need to have your formulas visible unless you're troubleshooting something that isn't working.

Dialogue Box

I will sometimes reference a dialogue box. These are the boxes that occasionally pop up with additional options for you to choose from for that particular task. Usually I include a screen shot so you know what it should look like.

Paste Special – Values

I will sometimes suggest that you paste special-values. What this means is to paste your data using the Values option under Paste Options (the one with 123 on the clipboard). This will paste the values from the cells you copied without also bringing over any of the formulas that created those values.

Dropdown

I will occasionally refer to a dropdown or dropdown menu. This is generally a list of potential choices that you can select from. The existence of the list is indicated by an arrow next to the first available selection. I will occasionally refer to the list of options you see when you click on a dropdown arrow as the dropdown menu.

ABOUT THE AUTHOR

M.L. Humphrey is a former stockbroker with a degree in Economics from Stanford and an MBA from Wharton who has spent close to twenty years as a regulator and consultant in the financial services industry.

You can reach M.L. at mlhumphreywriter@gmail.com or at mlhumphrey.com.

www.ingramcontent.com/pod-product-compliance
Lightning Source LLC
LaVergne TN
LVHW052126070326
832902LV00038B/3956